Samson

A Type of the Church

Samson

A Type of the Church

by
David Crank

Harrison House
Tulsa, Oklahoma

Unless otherwise noted, all Scripture quotations are taken from the *King James Version* of the Bible.

Samson: A Type of the Church
ISBN 0-89274-864-8
Copyright © 1991 by David Crank
David Crank Ministries
1416 Larkin Williams Road
St. Louis, Missouri 63026

Special Dedication

* To my heavenly Father Who has been so eternally patient with me.

* To my earthly, spiritual fathers whom the Holy Spirit has used to change my life: Kenneth Hagin, Kenneth Copeland, and Jerry Savelle.

* To my precious, one-of-a-kind wife, Sharon.

* To the Holy Spirit Who knows me and still loves me.

* To Carlton D. Pearson whose friendship and ministry have been like apples of gold in settings of silver.

* To Richard and Lindsay Roberts whose personal graciousness to Sharon and me has been a wonderful example of the gifts of the Spirit, and the fruits of the Spirit.

Biography

 **David Crank** was a St. Louis County police officer for five years and spent two years as a juvenile officer. He served three years in U.S. Army security and held a top secret crypto-clearance. He is a graduate of the Missouri Highway Patrol Academy.

David was born again while watching Christian television and was filled with the Holy Spirit in a police squad car.

David and his wife Sharon began the full-time ministry on the evangelistic field over a decade ago. They have ministered nationally and internationally.

David has developed a large teaching center in southwest St. Louis County, and his ministry has received national acclaim through uncompromised teaching and preaching of the Word of God.

David has a nationwide ministry in teaching tapes and has a radio ministry Monday through Friday. In July 1984, David started taping for television in his 2,000-seat auditorium. David refers to the new auditorium as a Spiritual Production Center.

On July 14, 1984, the "DAVID CRANK PRESENTS" television program premiered on a local St. Louis television station. In less than 30 days, the program was on stations in many major cities. In October 1984, "DAVID CRANK PRESENTS" began to be broadcast via satellite, and the program began airing in all 50 states and many foreign countries. In March 1985, the program was expanded to a daily format, and is now seen twice a day, prime time across the country. David feels that the medium of television, by using the latest state of the art equipment and satellite technology, is one of the greatest tools God has given him to reach the entire world.

David stands in the offices of prophet and teacher and ministers under a heavy anointing. God uses him mightily in all phases of his ministry.

In July 1984, God opened special doors for David's ministry. David was interviewed for television by Kenneth Copeland at the East Coast Believer's Convention. Also, in July 1984, David met personally with Rev. Oral Roberts, in a special five-hour meeting at the ORU campus in Tulsa, Oklahoma, and has appeared on Oral Roberts' Sunday program, "Expect a Miracle." David is a frequent guest on Richard Roberts' television program and has conducted financial seminars and healing crusades with Richard and Lindsay Roberts at Oral Roberts University and in other states.

Contents

Foreword

In life, what you compromise to get you usually lose in the final analysis. And God's Word to you today is not a compromising word, but instead a word of power.

It is the day to put on the sevenfold armor of God. It is the hour of spiritual warfare. It is the time to . . . seek first the kingdom of God and His righteousness, and all these things (things we need for our lives) will be added unto us.

God's powerful Word to the Body of Christ is . . . to rise, to shine, for His light is come . . . (Is. 60:1). Jesus is our Savior. Jesus is our Healer. Jesus is our Deliverer. Jesus is our Lord of all.

In this book written by David Crank is the story of how a man named Samson heard from God, how he got into disobedience and missed God's plan for his life, and how he ultimately repented and came back to God.

It is a powerful story in the Scriptures because it brings to light much of what has gone on in the churches, as well as what is going on now and what is to come. I believe it will be a blessing to you.

David Crank, pastor of Faith Christian World Outreach Center in St. Louis, Missouri, has been a long-time friend to ORU and the Roberts family. He is a man full of faith and the Holy Spirit. This book will stimulate your faith and help bring you into a position to obey God in all the things He has impressed you to do.

I am praying that it will minister to you as it has ministered to me.

Richard Roberts

Introduction

Samson — A Type of the Church came as a word to the Body of Christ through the gift of prophecy. It came supernaturally in the heat of all the "scandals" of some ministries in the winding down of the decade of the 80s.

The Lord prophesied through me that He was purging and cleaning house. Of course, the devil being the devil tried to capitalize on it and merchandise it. Getting back to the main point, God prophesied through me during a Sunday night healing rally in 1988. I prohesied concerning the Church being a type of Samson and how Samson missed God in some areas.

Samson (a type of the Church) ended up with his eyes being poked out and pushing the grinding wheel as the world laughed and scoffed. We the godly found ourselves in a very similar situation in the winding down of the 80s. We were the *butt* of every "comic" comedian's joke. But the Good News is, thank God there's always Good News. As the Lord spoke through me, Samson (a type of the Church) had broken three vows, one being a Nazarite vow — he could never shave his head.

In the book of First Corinthians it speaks of our hair as being a type of our glory. The prophecy went on to say (*glory to God*) that as the world was laughing and scoffing at the Church, what they and the devil didn't notice was that our hair (*our glory*) was growing back.

I can hardly write because my spirit is leaping within me. All of our hair will soon be back. I say to you as a prophet and teacher in the Body of Christ, this is the decade that we — Samson (a type of the Church) — will push over the pillars of the devil in the greatest move of signs, wonders, and miracles that the world has ever known.

The devil is so blind and has always overplayed his hand. I testify to you that the Holy Spirit said to me, ''The little boy that led blind Samson (a type of the Church) was a type of none other than God, the Holy Ghost (a little child shall lead them).''

The Spirit of the Lord is saying to me for the Body of Christ to fasten their seat belts, for the ministry of the 90s shall be the *decade of the Holy Ghost.*

David Crank

1

Time to Seek the Lord

In 1988, I prophesied by utterance of the Holy
Ghost that Samson is a type of the Church of Jesus
Christ. Like the Church of today, Samson missed God.
He grieved the Lord. He did not keep his vows. As
a result, he ended up in prison, his head shorn, his
body in chains, his energy spent in grinding out grain
like an animal. His enemies, the Philistines (a type of
the world), had gouged out his eyes and made sport
of him.

The good news at the end of that prophecy was
that God said that Samson's hair (which represents the
glory of the Lord) was beginning to grow back out.

In other words, what the Lord was saying is that
His glory will return to the Church before Jesus Christ
returns to earth for His Body.

We need the glory of God back in the Church
today.

The Glory of the Lord

The root word from which *glory* is taken is the
word *glow*. We Christians need this glow about us if
we are to shine forth as children of light and draw
others to Christ and His Church. As Jesus said, **Ye are
the light of the world. A city that is set on a hill cannot
be hid** (Matt. 5:14). We are not to hide our candle

under a bushel, but to let it shine forth to give light to all those in darkness. (vv. 15,16.)

To glow, to give light, to show forth the glory of God, we must do the works of our Lord, and even "greater works than these." (John 14:12.) We need to see people come up out of their wheelchairs. We need to see blind eyes opened, and deaf ears unstopped. We cannot make such things happen in and of ourselves. It will take the work of the Holy Spirit within us. We are channels of God's life and power, but it is the Lord Himself Who is the Healer.

In Hebrew, the word *Samson* means "little sun" or "light." In the New Testament, Jesus called Himself "the light of the world." (John 8:12.) He also said that as children of God that is what we are to be.

What's in a Name?

In the Old Testament, when people prayed and asked God for a child, they inquired of the Lord what the child was going to be like. Many times God answered by giving them a name for that child which described his nature or the role he was to fulfill. God will still do that for us today if we will ask Him.

In days of old there seemed to be more respect for God. Older people's names were Bible names. My mother named me after David, which in Hebrew means "beloved." She chose a biblical name because she loved the Bible. My brother was named Stephen, after the evangelist of that name. My sister, Ruth, was also given a Bible name. The Bible used to mean something to God's people.

I am not being critical of anyone whose name is not taken from the Bible. I am simply making an observation. I am using this example to illustrate how people used to be more mindful of God and the things of God than they are now.

Being God-Minded

In Colossians 3:1,2 the Apostle Paul writes to believers:

> **If ye then be risen with Christ, seek those things which are above, where Christ sitteth on the right hand of God.**
>
> **Set your affection on things above, not on things on the earth.**

We Christians are to be "God-minded." We are to keep our minds and hearts on the Lord and the things of His Kingdom. If we show little esteem for God and His Kingdom, He will show little esteem for us and our world. It is time we believers quit esteeming God little and start esteeming Him big!

The Coming Judgment

I believe with all my heart that we are at the end of the Church age. I believe God is consummating the end of the age right now. We have never lived in such a time as this.

In 1982, the Lord spoke to me and said that judgment would soon begin. I shared that message with my congregation. However, I had no idea then of the full extent of that coming judgment. I only knew that the Lord said it would be awesome. He declared that everything that could be shaken would be shaken.

Since 1983, the situation has progressively worsened. I believe there will never again be an hour in which we in the Church can carry on business as usual or in which we can sit on our righteous indignation and do nothing before God. No longer can we believers content ourselves with sitting in church, yawning, and wondering when 12 o'clock will come so we can get up and go home. No longer can we watch six hours of television a day, then give God 15 minutes (or less) of our time, and wonder why we don't live but die.

Even if you and I are not in the fivefold ministry, we, as believers, are priests before God. (1 Pet. 2:9.) His Word says, **Let the priests, the ministers of the Lord, weep between the porch and the altar, and let them say, Spare thy people, O Lord...** (Joel 2:17).

...Shall the earth be made to bring forth in one day? or shall a nation be born at once? asks the Lord in Isaiah 66:8, **for as soon as Zion travailed, she brought forth her children.** It is by travailing, in prayer and intercession, that children are brought forth into the Kingdom of God.

One way to hear from God is to take hold of the altar with travail in earnest intercession and prayer, with groanings which cannot be uttered. (Rom. 8:26.)

The Apostle Peter warns us, **Be sober, be vigilant; because your adversary the devil, as a roaring lion, walketh about, seeking whom he may devour** (1 Pet. 5:8).

There has never been a time when satanic activity has been on the rise to the degree that it is right now. I believe this is happening because Satan knows that

18

his time is short. He knows that his reign is almost over. His tyranny over the lives of men and women, boys and girls, is about to come to an end. Death, and all the rest of the devil's filth and garbage, is about to be done away with.

The Return of Jesus

The Lord Jesus says of His imminent return, **...behold, I come quickly; and my reward is with me...**(Rev. 22:12).

If you don't know exactly when Jesus will return, that ought to encourage you to keep your heart and mind pure. These are the last days. Jesus can come whenever He wants. The last thing that literally had to be fulfilled before Jesus could return was the blossoming of the fig tree, and that took place in 1947. He can now come whenever He wishes.

The Lord of the Flies

A church leader in days past had a major heart attack and died. He had attended church regularly and had taught a Sunday school class, but in his own words, he was a "hypocrite." He was not right with God.

When this man died, God showed him heaven and hell. He was never allowed on the inside of heaven, but he saw the people who had died at the same time he had passed away. An angel stood at his side and had him watch as less than 25 percent of those who had died that day went into the kingdom of heaven.

19

When I read those statistics, immediately I thought of Matthew 7:14 in which Jesus told His disciples, **...strait is the gate, and narrow is the way, which leadeth unto life, and few there be that find it.**

I thought: what a staggering, awesome thing. The man was actually at the gate of heaven. His spirit had left his body, but the Lord gave him another chance so he could go on living and teach and warn people around the world. He came back to life and got right with God. Then he began to share with others what he had seen and heard. In his out-of-body experience, the Lord showed him all kinds of devils, what they look like, and the different levels of demonic powers.

A few years ago I had an open vision in which I saw hell belch forth what looked like billions of flies. I later discovered that Beelzebub, one of the biblical names of the devil, means "the lord of the flies." Satan is the king of the flies.

The flies I saw in my vision made their way all around the United States of America and then headed for other nations of the world. I now believe that what I saw was the attack which the Body of Christ has been currently experiencing.

If we believers are not careful we will succumb to apostasy, coldness of heart, and lethargy. It is time we stir ourselves. This is the hour to turn our minds toward God, to seek Him with all our hearts, to give Him first place in our lives, and to do exactly what He says. Then it will be well with us, and we will escape that which is to come.

The Shaking of the Church and the World

In 1982, while I was in Tennessee attending a revival led by a brother in Christ, Jesus walked into my room and said to me, "After I finish cleaning up the Church, I will turn to the world. The shaking of the Church will not be anything compared to the way I will deal with the world."

When I think of how tough it has been for the Body of Christ these past few years, I wonder what it is going to be like for the world. God will shake it until people's teeth rattle.

But for us in the Church, the time of shaking has now become the time of seeking.

2
Samson: A Man of the Vow

In Bondage to the Philistines

Let's look at this account in Judges 13, beginning with some background information about the situation which existed in Israel at the time this event took place:

> And the children of Israel did evil again in the sight of the Lord; and the Lord delivered them into the hand of the Philistines forty years.
>
> **Judges 13:1**

God didn't put the Israelites into the hand of the Philistines. The children of Israel put themselves into Philistine bondage.

Whenever God's people get out of His will, they end up in the hands of the enemy. If you and I are not careful to remain in obedience to the Lord, we will end up at the mercy of some devil or under the influence of a demonic spirit rather than under the power and control of the Holy Spirit.

The Calling of a Nazarite

> And there was a certain man of Zorah, of the family of the Danites, whose name was Manoah; and his wife was barren, and bare not.
>
> And the angel of the Lord appeared unto the woman, and said unto her, Behold now, thou art barren, and barest not: but thou shalt conceive, and bear a son.

> Now therefore beware, I pray thee, and drink not wine nor strong drink, and eat not any unclean thing:
>
> For, lo, thou shalt conceive, and bear a son; and no razor shall come on his head: for the child shall be a Nazarite unto God from the womb: and he shall begin to deliver Israel out of the hand of the Philistines.
>
> Judges 13:2-5

In Hebrew, the word translated *Nazarite* is *nazir*, which means "unshorn" (as of hair) or "unpruned" (as of a vine). It is derived from another Hebrew word *nazar* which means "to hold aloof," "to abstain," or "to separate." Another variant of this word is *nezer*, which is used to refer to something set apart by dedication. The angel told Samson's mother that her child was to be a Nazarite, one set apart and dedicated to the Lord. As a Nazarite, Samson was to be a person of the vow. (Num. 6.)

Preparation of a Nazarite

So the Lord began to prepare a man to serve and represent Him. He began His preparation of this man from his conception, telling His mother that he would be a Nazarite from the womb:

> For, lo, thou shalt conceive, and bear a son....
>
> Then the woman came and told her husband, saying, A man of God came unto me....
>
> ...he said unto me, Behold, thou shalt conceive, and bear a son; and now drink no wine nor strong drink, neither eat any unclean thing: for the child shall be a Nazarite to God from the womb to the day of his death.
>
> And the angel of the Lord said unto Manoah, Of all that I said unto the woman let her beware.

24

> **She may not eat of any thing that cometh of the vine, neither let her drink wine or strong drink, nor eat any unclean thing: all that I commanded her let her observe.**
>
> Judges 13:5-7,13,14

Now I don't believe this repetition was included in the Bible just to make a "fat" book instead of a "skinny" one. The Lord sent the angel to deliver the same message to Manoah that had been spoken to his wife. Then the Holy Spirit moved upon the writer of the book of Judges to record it in the Bible so *we* wouldn't forget it. We must keep these things before our eyes and in our hearts, or else we will find ourselves in compromise.

In some ministries and churches today, it seems that the lamp of God is being turned down. Many believers act as if they don't want to make waves or cause a stir. They give the impression that they don't want their names in the newspaper or their pictures on television. They shy away from any words or actions that might call attention to themselves or their God.

Although I agree that we are to avoid *negative* publicity that will bring disgrace to the Lord and harm to His Church, I still think that God wants us to cast out devils and to wail in intercession before Him on behalf of others. I believe He still wants to hear the sound of a rushing mighty wind among His people, as on the day of Pentecost. (Acts 2:2.)

God needs a "man" in the earth today, and you and I are his "man" and His "woman" in this world. We are the Body of Christ, and we have a Head, Who is Christ.

The Arrival and Work of a Nazarite

At God's appointed time, Samson arrived on the scene:

And the woman bare a son, and called his name Samson: and the child grew, *and the Lord blessed him.*
Judges 13:24

When he was grown, Samson became the fourteenth judge of Israel between the time of the death of Joshua and the beginning of the reign of Saul as the first king of Israel. The Hebrew word translated *judge* in the Old Testament is *shaphet* and comes from a root word meaning "to judge" or "to pronounce sentence." In the New Testament, the Greek word is *krites*, which was used to refer to a civil magistrate or one in judicial authority.

As God's "judges" (His magistrates), we believers are to be the ones in authority over the powers, princes, and rulers of darkness. We are to keep the devil bound. We are to be God's "Samsons." We are children of light. We are to be the ones who bind and loose in the earth. The devil knows who has authority over him. He knows where sins abound, and he knows where to find compromise. We must be full of the Holy Ghost to take and use the authority Jesus has given us as His representatives in this world.

These judges of Israel were charismatic leaders, raised up by God to be Israel's saviors. They were especially endowed by the Spirit of God to do the work to which He had called them. In reality, they were primarily military deliverers, raised up for the express purpose of saving the people of Israel from the oppression of foreign powers. During the period of the judges, times were extremely distressing. It was a cruel, barbarous, and bloody period in the history of Israel, perhaps not unlike the perilous times in which we live today.

The Vow of the Nazarite

The Nazarite vow was a perpetual vow.

In some circles the Nazarites were called "people of the vow." Unlike eunuchs, however, Nazarites were under no obligation to remain unmarried. Jesus said concerning marriage and the blessings and requirements of it:

> ...All men cannot receive this saying, save they to whom it is given.
>
> For there are some eunuchs, which were so born from their mother's womb: and there are some eunuchs, which were made eunuchs of men: and there be eunuchs, which have made themselves eunuchs for the kingdom of heaven's sake. He that is able to receive it, let him receive it.
>
> Matthew 19:11,12

But while a Nazarite was under no obligation to remain celibate, there were three distinct limitations placed upon him by the Nazarite vow (Num. 6.):

1. The renunciation of any and all products of the vine.

2. The prohibition against the use of the razor on his head (no haircuts).

3. The avoidance of contact with any dead body (carcass or corpse).

The Lord blessed Samson. As he matured into manhood, his hair grew out and the anointing of the Lord upon him increased. I believe Samson's parents raised him right. I believe that, like Jesus, he **increased**

27

in wisdom and stature, and in favour with God and man (Luke 2:52).

When God's blessings begin to flow upon a person, as they did with Samson, it can be a time of great danger. If that individual's attention is not kept focused on the Lord, if he does not exercise care to keep his motives pure, he can fall into sin and error. When things are going well, sometimes it is easy to relax a bit and become careless and prideful, which can lead to temptation and compromise.

3

Samson:
An Exact Type of the Church

Jesus, the Head of the Church, was born supernaturally, and His birth was declared by an angel. Samson, too, was born supernaturally. His birth was also announced by an angel. Samson, like Jesus, grew in the nurture and admonition of the Lord.

Samson's mother was barren, and an angel spoke to his father, Manoah, and gave him some instructions about the son he was to sire.

"You are going to have a son," the angel said. "He is to be a Nazarite from his birth." His mother named him *Samson*, which means "little sun" or "light."

Qualification for God's Call

God has always had a man to represent Him in the earth. The children of Israel were in bondage, not for 40 years, but for 400 years. God heard their lament in Goshen and raised up a man by the name of Moses. Now Moses was very humble and said to God, "Lord, who am I to speak for You? I stutter and stammer. I can't even talk plainly."

To reassure him, the Lord said to Moses, "I will use what is at your disposal."

"What is that in your hand?" the Lord asked Moses.

"Nothing but a stick," Moses responded.

"Throw it down," commanded the Lord.

When Moses did as he was ordered, the stick turned into a snake. Then God said, "Pick it up." As Moses lifted up the serpent by the tail, it became a stick again.

This should be a lesson for all of us. God will use what is in our hands, if we will let Him. He is not looking for great natural talent or professional ability. He is looking for dedication and availability, for people who will do what He says.

Who does God have upon the earth today? He has us! You and me! We are the light of the world today. Some members of the Body of Christ have grown dim in this hour and are no longer the bright and shining beacons they should be. But we are the only earthly instruments God has at His disposal to carry forth His light and truth. I am glad He is a faith-God, and I am glad He doesn't waver.

Samson as a Type of the Church

Samson was born in Zorah, a city about 15 miles west of Jerusalem on the borders of Judah and Dan. He was an Israelite of the tribe of Dan. This tribe had been given the fertile area lying between Judah and the Mediterranean Sea, which was occupied by the Philistines. This is perhaps the reason the Philistines were Samson's major enemies.

Just as Samson's birth was supernatural, so also is the birth of the Body of Christ, **Which were born,**

not of blood, nor of the will of the flesh, nor of the will of man, but of God (John 1:13). We Christians came into existence as a body of believers as a result of the will of the Father.

Samson's birth was also a direct result of the will of God for the people of Israel. It was a command of God that Samson be different, set apart from others, consecrated to the Lord from birth to death — a Nazarite, a man of the vow.

4
Heated Flesh:
The Stage for Compromise

And Samson went down to *Timnath*, and saw a woman in Timnath of the daughters of the Philistines.
Judges 14:1

In Hebrew the word Timnath means "a holding in check."[1] Timnath was "a place of check." I will never be convinced that Samson stepped over the corporate limits into the Philistine city, the place of the check, without sensing a check from the Spirit of God in his own spirit.

Samson grew and God blessed him. He flexed his bulging "Pentecostal muscles" and recalled the exploits of his youth. But the mistake he made was that he went past the check.

The Danger of Ignoring the Check

The spirit of man is the candle of the Lord, searching all the inward parts of the belly.
Proverbs 20:27

Samson began to cool to his vows, but heat up to his flesh.

---

[1]Herbert Lockyer, Sr., *Nelson Illustrated Dictionary* (Nashville: Thomas Nelson, 1986), p. 1052.

At one time or another, every man, woman, boy, or girl has headed toward something or has decided to do something that seemed so appealing to the mind and the body! The flesh wanted it, but on the inside, in the spirit realm, there was a check.

The Lord has told us, . . . **I will never leave thee, nor forsake thee** (Heb. 13:5). Whether we are aware of it or not, the Spirit of the Lord resides within us and seeks to communicate with us every moment of the day. We may not heed the authoritative voice of the indwelling Holy Spirit. We may choose to ignore it. But we do so at our own peril.

God will speak to us in and through our spirit. Never violate your own spirit. When that inward check is felt, stop. Don't do as Samson did and go stubbornly ahead with your plans and intentions regardless of what the Lord is trying to tell you. Driven by the power of his own lustful desires, Samson ignored the voice of the Lord and wound up in serious trouble.

Remember, desire and lust are driving forces. Don't yield to them. Don't step across that line. Samson did, and stepped out of the Lord's will and protection and right into his first compromise.

No one is led into a compromising situation overnight. It is always the result of a series of steps in the wrong direction. It begins with a thought, just a bit of mental compromise. Then, like Samson, step by step the person is led to actually commit the act which he has been contemplating in his mind and heart.

No one becomes an embezzler by stealing a huge amount of money all at once. It usually begins with a little thing. Perhaps taking a pencil home from the office. Gradually petty thievery leads to bigger and bigger heists. The end result is full-fledged embezzlement.

The Holy Spirit is within us to check us when we first begin to even contemplate a wrong step. He will always warn us about wrongdoing because He is the Spirit of truth. God is a righteous God. He is a clean God, a holy God. He expects His children to be as He is.

The Word of God asks:

> Who shall ascend into the hill of the Lord? or who shall stand in his holy place?
>
> He that hath clean hands, and a pure heart; who hath not lifted up his soul unto vanity, nor sworn deceitfully.
>
> He shall receive the blessing from the Lord, and righteousness from the God of his salvation.
>
> **Psalm 24:3-5**

So Samson went down to Timnath ("the place of the check"). He went against the check of the Spirit of God within his own spirit. There he "saw a woman in Timnath of the daughters of the Philistines."

Samson's Mistake

> And he came up, and told his father and his mother, and said, I have seen a woman in Timnath of the daughters of the Philistines: now therefore get her for me to wife.
>
> **Judges 14:2**

The Bible says, **Be ye not unequally yoked together with unbelievers...**(2 Cor. 6:14). Samson knew this godly principle, but he chose to ignore it.

He went to the place of the check and fell into temptation. He saw a Philistine woman who was lustrous and infatuating. He followed the heat of his flesh rather than the warning of the Lord.

We must beware of making Samson's mistake. We must always follow the leading of the Lord, not the lusts of our heated flesh or our carnal desires. We must be careful not to cross the checkpoint in our spirit, because Satan always has something prepared for us to deceive and destroy us.

Samson's Stubbornness

Why didn't Samson find a wife in the camp of Judah? Even his own father and mother asked him:

> ...Is there never a woman among the daughters of thy brethren, or among all my people, that thou goest to take a wife of the uncircumcised Philistines? And Samson said unto his father, Get her for me; for she pleaseth me well.
>
> **Judges 14:3**

Samson was stubborn and headstrong. He wanted his own way. He was willing to compromise in order to fulfill his own carnal desires. And one compromise always leads to another.

Samson's First Compromise

> **Then went Samson down, and his father and his mother, to Timnath** (the place of the check)**, and came to the vineyards of Timnath....**
>
> **Judges 14:5**

God had warned Samson, "Keep away from wine and strong drink." But Samson did not heed this warning. He purposely went down to Timnath, "and came to the vineyards."

Now those vines were not grown to produce Kool-Aid! They were grown to produce wine and strong drink. In fact, Timnath was the largest producer of grapes and wine in the whole Philistine area. Despite God's warning, Samson was right in the middle of "the place of the vine." This was his first compromise. He violated the first prohibition of the Nazarite vow.

Samson and the Lion

Then went Samson down....and came to the vineyards of Timnath: and, behold, a young lion roared against him.

And the Spirit of the Lord came mightily upon him, and he rent him as he would have rent a kid, and he had nothing in his hand: but he told not his father or his mother what he had done.

Judges 14:5,6

Why didn't Samson tell his parents what he had done? The answer is revealed in verse 7.

And he went down, and talked with the woman; and she pleased Samson well.

So Samson talked with the Philistine woman, but withheld information from his own parents.

Why then did the Spirit of God still come upon Samson? Why did the anointing continue to rest upon him? Because the gifts and calling of God are without repentance. (Rom. 11:29.) However, that calling will not remain there for perpetuity if a person continues to grieve the Spirit of the Lord.

God will dwell and dwell and deal and deal, for a certain amount of time, but if we bullheadedly proceed in opposition to God's commands, at some point the anointing will begin to wane. We must maintain fidelity in order to keep the gifts and calling that God has placed upon us.

Samson's Second Compromise

And after a time he returned to take her, and he turned aside to see the carcase of the lion: and, behold, there was a swarm of bees and honey in the carcase of the lion.

And he took thereof in his hands, and went on eating, and came to his father and mother, and he gave them, and they did eat: but he told not them that he had taken the honey out of the carcase of the lion.

Judges 14:8,9

Samson's first compromise was going to the place of the vine or the place of strong drink. This compromise led to his becoming involved in fornication.

Samson killed the young lion which "roared against him" at the vineyards. Just as Samson faced the lion, so we must face the wiles of the enemy if we get into compromise. Satan has something prepared for us which we will have to deal with when we step into his territory. Although we may not recognize the danger or realize its importance, Satan has a plan for everything he does.

While Samson was involved with the Philistine woman he had chosen to marry, he turned aside to see the remains of the lion he had slain. There he discovered a swarm of bees in the carcass of the dead animal. Watching the bees drew Samson's attention to their honey. He looked into the lion he had slain and decided to enjoy the sweetness of his kill. When Samson reached down to get the honey out of the lion's belly, he touched its dead body. This was the second vow he had broken!

You and I can preserve our own lives by not violating the check in our spirit. Something may look innocent — an association, a business deal, a person. We may not understand what is wrong with the situation, but the Lord will warn us through a check in our spirit. To ignore that check is to court danger and destruction.

Friend, Satan has a plan to "ditch" you and me. He has an ulterior motive and a hidden purpose for everything he does. For Samson, the devil's plan was to entice and tempt him with carnal desire. First it was the Philistine woman, and now it is the sweetness of the honey.

The devil often uses something desirable to seduce and destroy. He will present something to us that we desire. Like Samson, we will reach down to take it. While we are reaching for that thing, we will break a vow. We will compromise.

Why didn't Samson tell his parents where the honey had come from and how he had obtained it? Because he was ashamed. Why did the Holy Spirit have this information put in the Bible for us to read? So that we, when we read it today, thousands of years later, would know that Samson had a check in his spirit. Samson didn't tell his parents because he knew he had violated his vow and his own heart.

Heated flesh will always lead to compromise, and it will also set the stage for defeat and despair. Momentary gratification produces long-term heartache!

Samson Betrayed

So his father went down unto the woman: and Samson made there a feast; for so used the young men to do.

And it came to pass, when they saw him, that they brought thirty companions to be with him.

And Samson said unto them, I will now put forth a riddle unto you: if ye can certainly declare it me within the seven days of the feast, and find it out, then I will give you thirty sheets and thirty change of garments:

But if ye cannot declare it me, then shall ye give me thirty sheets and thirty change of garments. And they said unto him, Put forth thy riddle, that we may hear it.

And he said unto them, Out of the eater came forth meat, and out of the strong came forth sweetness. And they could not in three days expound the riddle.

And it came to pass on the seventh day, that they said unto Samson's wife, Entice thy husband, that he may declare unto us the riddle, lest we burn thee and thy father's house with fire: have ye called us to take that we have? is it not so?

And Samson's wife wept before him, and said, Thou dost but hate me, and lovest me not: thou hast put forth a riddle unto the children of my people, and hast not told it me. And he said unto her, Behold, I have not told it my father nor my mother, and shall I tell it thee?

And she wept before him the seven days, while their feast lasted: and it came to pass on the seventh day, that he told her, because she lay sore upon him: and she told the riddle to the children of her people.

And the men of the city said unto him on the seventh day before the sun went down, What is sweeter than honey? and what is stronger than a lion?

And he said unto them, If ye had not plowed with my heifer, ye had not found out my riddle.

And the Spirit of the Lord came upon him, and he went down to Ashkelon, and slew thirty men of them, and took their spoil, and gave change of garments unto them which expounded the riddle. And his anger was kindled, and he went up to his father's house.

But Samson's wife was given to his companion, whom he used as his friend.

Judges 14:10-20

Samson's unequal marriage did not work out. The Philistine woman who became his wife betrayed him to his enemies, her own people. She ended up becoming the wife of Samson's best man.

This should be a lesson to us all. What we compromise to get, we will eventually lose. Always!

5

Samson's Anger
Stirs the Enemy Camp

But it came to pass within a while after, in the time of wheat harvest, that Samson visited his wife with a kid; and he said, I will go in to my wife into the chamber. But her father would not suffer him to go in.

And her father said, I verily thought that thou hadst utterly hated her; therefore I gave her to thy companion: is not her younger sister fairer than she? take her, I pray thee, instead of her.

And Samson said concerning them, Now shall I be more blameless than the Philistines, though I do them a displeasure.

And Samson went and caught three hundred foxes, and took firebrands, and turned tail to tail, and put a firebrand in the midst between two tails.

And when he had set the brands on fire, he let them go into the standing corn of the Philistines, and burnt up both the shocks, and also the standing corn, with the vineyards and olives.

Judges 15:1-5

Like Samson, we may have a call of God upon our lives, but if we give into our fleshly desires or human emotions we may still make a wrong decision, as Samson did here. Although we are God's chosen instruments in the earth, we can still make a wrong move, step out of God's wisdom, and thereby open the door to all kinds of trouble and misery that God never intended for us.

Samson Stirs the Enemy Camp

Then the Philistines said, Who hath done this? And they answered, Samson, the son in law of the Timnite, because he had taken his wife, and given her to his companion. And the Philistines came up, and burnt her and her father with fire.

And Samson said unto them, Though ye have done this, yet will I be avenged of you, and after that I will cease.

And he smote them hip and thigh with a great slaughter: and he went down and dwelt in the top of the rock Etam.

Judges 15:6-8

Samson's actions angered the entire Philistine army. They killed Samson's wife and his father-in-law and set out to capture Samson in order to take vengeance upon him for what he had done. So by giving in to his anger and his lust for revenge, Samson created a strong feeling of animosity against him among the enemies of his people.

Samson Stirs His Own People

Then the Philistines went up, and pitched in Judah, and spread themselves in Lehi.

And the men of Judah said, Why are ye come up against us? And they answered, To bind Samson are we come up, to do to him as he hath done to us.

And three thousand men of Judah went to the top of the rock Etam, and said to Samson, Knowest thou not that the Philistines are rulers over us? what is this that thou hast done unto us? And he said unto them, As they did unto me, so have I done unto them.

> And they said unto him, We are come down to bind thee, that we may deliver thee into the hand of the Philistines. And Samson said unto them, Swear unto me, that ye will not fall upon me yourselves.
>
> And they spake unto him, saying, No; but we will bind thee fast, and deliver thee into their hand: but surely we will not kill thee. And they bound him with two new cords, and brought him up from the rock.
>
> Judges 15:9-13

So because of his rash actions, Samson's own countrymen came against him. The Philistines put pressure on Judah, so in order to appease their masters, the men of Judah came out to locate and capture Samson and turn him over to the enemy. And Samson agreed to go with them without doing them any harm.

Samson's Pride Displayed

> And when he came unto Lehi, the Philistines shouted against him: and the Spirit of the Lord came mightily upon him, and the cords that were upon his arms became as flax that was burnt with fire, and his bands loosed from off his hands.
>
> And he found a new jawbone of an ass (a donkey), and put forth his hand, and took it, and slew a thousand men therewith.
>
> And Samson said, With the jawbone of an ass, heaps upon heaps, with the jaw of an ass have I slain a thousand men.
>
> Judges 15:14-16

"With the jaw of an ass have I slain a thousand men."

Do you notice any bragging here? Samson is getting out of line. He is becoming bragadocious and prideful instead of humbly acknowledging that his great strength and ability are from the Lord.

We in the Church must beware of thinking and acting as if our great accomplishments are a result of our own ability, power, or virtue. We must be on our guard against falling into pride and conceit by thinking that we don't need anybody, that we can do it all by ourselves.

Proverbs 16:18 warns us, **Pride goeth before destruction, and an haughty spirit before a fall.**

Do you sense Samson's wrong attitude here in this passage? It is not the attitude that we should have before the Lord or display to the world. We must always be careful to give glory to God, not to ourselves.

Samson Calls Upon the Lord

And it came to pass, when he had made an end of speaking, that he cast away the jawbone out of his hand, and called that place Ramath-lehi (jawbone hill).

And he was sore athirst, and called on the Lord, and said, Thou hast given this great deliverance into the hand of thy servant: and now shall I die for thirst, and fall into the hand of the uncircumcised?

But God clave an hollow place that was in the jaw, and there came water thereout; and when he had drunk, his spirit came again, and he revived: wherefore he called the name thereof En-hakkore (caller's spring), **which is in Lehi unto this day.**

And he judged Israel in the days of the Philistines twenty years.

Judges 15:17-20

When Samson realized he was in trouble, he called upon the Lord Who heard his cry and miraculously provided him water out of the very weapon he had used against his enemies.

The Lord will do the same for us, when we fall into sin and error, if we will humbly repent and turn to Him in faith and confidence. We too will judge and rule with Him as long as we remain in submission to His Word and His will.

6

Samson Meets His Match!

Then went Samson to Gaza, and saw there an harlot, and went in unto her.

Judges 16:1

In Hebrew the word *Gaza* means "stronghold."[1]

One sin leads to another. First Samson went to Timnath, a place of check. Then he went to the vineyards of Timnath, a place of the vine. Now he goes to Gaza, a strong place, a "stronghold."

No longer is Samson in a place of check, a place of compromise, but he is in Gaza, the capital city of strongholds. It is here that Satan begins to build a stronghold in Samson's life.

Wrongdoing never pays: **Be not deceived; God is not mocked: for whatsoever a man soweth, that shall he also reap** (Gal. 6:7).

Plant a few seeds into pornography, fornication, and adultery, and you will reap the fruit of what you have sown: the stronghold of the enemy in these respective areas.

One sin, if not renounced, leads to another and another until it becomes a stronghold, just like a strong grip. If you go past the place of the check, you will end up in Gaza, the place of strongholds in your life.

---

[1]Lockyer, p. 407.

First of all, Samson saw a woman he desired and said to himself, "I am going to make everything right; I will marry her." The marriage was short-lived, however, because the bride was taken from him and given to his companion. Why did this happen? Because she was a Philistine, a pagan. Compromise led Samson to have relations with an outsider, a woman of the world. The result was trouble, anger, hatred, and heartache.

After that experience, instead of repenting and learning from it, Samson became vengeful and hardened in heart. He made no attempt to seek the will of the Lord and find a suitable wife among his own kind. Instead, he went to visit a prostitute he found in Gaza. The Bible indicates that he "went in unto her" (that is, that he had sex with her).

Samson Abuses His Anointing

And it was told the Gazites, saying, Samson is come hither. And they compassed him in, and laid wait for him all night in the gate of the city, and were quiet all the night, saying, In the morning, when it is day, we shall kill him.

And Samson lay till midnight, and arose at midnight, and took the doors of the gate of the city. . . .

Judges 16:2,3

In the Bible the words *gates* and *doors* usually represent the power or authority of a city. Samson lay with the harlot, then got up. Because he had the anointing of the Lord upon him, he took away the gates (the power and authority) of the city.

Just because the anointing of God is manifested in a person's life does not mean that the Lord is pleased with that individual or his attitude and actions. Neither is it a sign that the anointing will remain with him forever.

In our day some people, like Samson, abuse and misuse their anointing. Some use it to raise money. Some use it for vain purposes, treating it lightly, not respecting it. If something is abused and misused long enough, it will be lost. If you and I abuse our spouses or children long enough, we will lose them. In the same way, if the holy things of God are abused or misused, eventually they will be taken away.

It is a privilege to stand in the pulpit. It is a privilege to come into the house of the Lord. But that privilege must be properly respected, otherwise it will become our undoing.

Samson lay with a harlot. He disobeyed the law of the Lord. He abused his anointing. And in the end he paid for his sins and error.

Samson was a hearer of the Word only, and not a doer of the Word. Yet he thought the power and anointing of the Lord would remain upon him forever, despite his wrong attitude and actions. He was mistaken. Anyone who is a hearer only will end up, like Samson, in self-deception.

Satan's Plan for Samson

And it came to pass afterward, that he loved a woman in the valley of Sorek, whose name was Delilah.

Judges 16:4

Now here is the clincher. Here we see the first step in the unfolding of the perfect plan of Satan for the downfall and destruction of Samson — who was supposed to be the light, the judge, and the keeper of Israel, the one to lead them out of their bondage to the Philistines.

Samson went to Sorek and fell in love with a woman named Delilah. In Hebrew, the word *Sorek* means "a vine" or "vine stock," specifically the one which produces the richest variety of grapes. Thus, Sorek was "the place of the vine" or "the place of the choice stock." And it was there, in Sorek, in the place of the *"choice stock"* that Samson met the temptress Delilah.

In Hebrew, the word *Delilah* means "delicate one."[2] The *Twentieth Century* translation indicates that it means "foxy one" or "sensuous one."

A sensuous woman like Delilah knows how to work her wiles upon a man. She knows how to dress and walk to appeal to his carnal nature, how to use her physical charms to snare and entrap him. Delilah was both well-equipped and well-informed in how to seduce a man and entice him into doing her bidding. That was all part of Satan's plan for Samson.

Samson Toys With the Anointing

And the lords of the Philistines came up unto her, and said unto her, Entice him, and see wherein his great strength lieth, and by what means we may prevail against him, that we may bind him to afflict him: and we will give thee every one of us eleven hundred pieces of silver.

---

[2]*The Dake Bible*, p. 283, note C,© 1963 by Finis Jennings Dake.

> And Delilah said to Samson, Tell me, I pray thee,
> wherein thy great strength lieth, and wherewith thou
> mightest be bound to afflict thee.
>
> And Samson said unto her, If they bind me with
> seven green withs (thongs) that were never dried, then
> shall I be weak, and be as another man.
>
> Judges 16:5-7

Samson lied. It is impossible to lie and still fulfill
the will and purpose of God in life. But an even greater
concern than the lie was the fact that Samson had
begun toying with his godly anointing. He had
forgotten who he was and where he had come from.

When I was in the Library of Congress, I took a
picture of a plaque which read, *"When a nation forgets
its beginnings, it begins to decay."* Some people forget
their beginnings. They forget where they came from.
They forget where they were when God got hold of
them. They grow accustomed to God and to the things
of God and begin to treat them with little esteem.

That is a deadly mistake, as we will see in
Samson's case.

Samson and the Vines

> Then the lords of the Philistines brought up to
> her seven green withs which had not been dried, and
> she bound him with them.
>
> Now there were men lying in wait, abiding with
> her in the chamber. And she said unto him, The
> Philistines be upon thee, Samson. And he brake the
> withs, as a thread of tow (a piece of string) is broken
> when it toucheth the fire. So (the secret of) his strength
> was not known.
>
> Judges 16:8,9

53

You may be wondering how this could happen to Samson. How could he allow himself to be tricked into even discussing the source of his great strength?

Friend, God told us that Samson was in Sorek for a reason. He had been led there by the devil to be destroyed. Samson was down in the valley of Sorek, the valley of the vine, playing with a "false vine" instead of being up on the mountain where he belonged, fellowshipping with the True Vine! (John 15:1.)

I believe Samson was drunk. I am convinced he had passed out from drinking too much wine. I believe Delilah had fed him from the "choice vineyards" of Sorek. She had put his head in her lap and lulled him to sleep. Alcohol will cause a person to let down his defenses and do things he doesn't realize he is doing — or even remember later!

Samson Under Pressure

And Delilah said unto Samson, Behold, thou hast mocked me, and told me lies: now tell me, I pray thee, wherewith thou mightest be bound.

And he said unto her, If they bind me fast with new ropes that never were occupied, then shall I be weak, and be as another man.

Delilah therefore took new ropes, and bound him therewith, and said unto him, The Philistines be upon thee, Samson. And there were liers in wait abiding in the chamber. And he brake them from off his arms like a thread.

Judges 16:10-12

Delilah began to put pressure on Samson. Again he found it necessary to lie in order to keep his secret.

When you and I start to lie, to toy with sin, we are playing with fire. When we come under pressure, we may not mean to get into compromise, but the closer we get to sin, the greater the chance that we will succumb. With each lie Samson got a little closer to destruction.

Samson Lies One Final Time

And Delilah said unto Samson, Hitherto thou hast mocked me, and told me lies: tell me wherewith thou mightest be bound. And he said unto her, If thou weavest the seven locks of my head with the web.

And she fastened it with the pin, and said unto him, The Philistines be upon thee, Samson. And he awaked out of his sleep, and went away with the pin of the beam, and with the web.

Judges 16:13,14

Now Samson lies one final time. He comes very close to revealing the source of his strength. He tells Delilah that it has something to do with his hair.

Samson Delivers His Heart

And she said unto him, How canst thou say, I love thee, when thine heart is not with me? thou hast mocked me these three times, and hast not told me wherein thy great strength lieth.

And it came to pass, when she pressed him daily with her words, and urged him, so that his soul was vexed unto death;

That *he told her all his heart,* and said unto her, There hath not come a razor upon mine head; for I have been a Nazarite unto God from my mother's womb: if I be shaven, then my strength will go from me, and I shall become weak, and be like any other man.

Judges 16:15-17

Samson delivered his heart to Delilah. The Holy Spirit showed me that he was sincere in placing his trust in her. He told her *all of his heart*. After all, she had probably told him a million times, "I love you," though she had lied. They had an intimate relationship. Who would violate that?

A devil! A harlot! A whore! Proverbs 23:27 says, **For a whore is a deep ditch . . . .**

Even before his hair was cut and his strength taken away from him, Samson had become "like any other man." He had revealed the source of his strength. He had betrayed his anointing.

We Christians are not to be like "any other man." We don't need to look like the world. We don't need to think, speak or behave as the world does. We don't need to go the world's way, to follow the world's pattern, to have the world's divorce rate. We need to be a "peculiar people" — a special race set aside unto God, vessels "meet for the Master's use." (1 Pet. 2:9, 2 Tim. 2:21.)

Samson Lulled to Sleep

And when Delilah saw that he had told her all his heart, she sent and called for the lords of the Philistines, saying, Come up this once, for he hath shewed me all his heart. Then the lords of the Philistines came up unto her, and brought money in their hand.

And she made him sleep upon her knees . . . .
Judges 16:18,19

God spoke to me and told me that much of the Church today is in the lap of the world being lulled to sleep.

Dear God, we want to be like other people. We want to go to church on Saturday evenings so we can have Sunday to ourselves. We want to drink with the world. We want to hold dances in the church. We want to have Christian sex.

This happened in one church I know. It was a scandal. The church had to let people go because of their involvement in fornication and adultery.

Why do such things happen? Because people are not taught the Word of God. The Bible teaches that faith comes by hearing. (Rom. 10:17.) If the Bible is not taught, then people are easily deceived. If we don't stand for something, we will fall for anything.

Too many Christians today want to be like the world, to be like "other men." They don't want to be different. But the Bible says that we are to be **...a chosen generation, a royal priesthood, an holy nation, a peculiar people...**(1 Pet. 2:9) so that we may show forth the praises of God.

Samson Afflicted by Delilah

And she made him sleep upon her knees; and she called for a man, and she caused him to shave off the seven locks of his head; and she began to afflict him, and his strength went from him.

Judges 16:19

If Samson had just been asleep, he would undoubtedly have awakened at the sound of scissors clipping! I personally believe he was dead drunk. Otherwise, how could Delilah have begun to "afflict him"?

This is the end result of compromise.

The Spirit of God Departed

And she said, The Philistines be upon thèe, Samson. And he awoke out of his sleep, and said, I will go out as at other times before, and shake myself. And he wist not that the Lord (the Spirit of God) **was departed from him.**

Judges 16:20

Samson violated the third vow. In the Bible, the word *hair* represents glory. Samson, as a Nazarite, was under a vow never to allow a razor to touch his head, his hair, the glory of the Lord which rested upon him.

I believe there are churches today that are still singing, hollering, praising God, and carrying on their regular programs, yet without realizing that the word *Ichabod* has been written over their door. (*Ichabod* means "the glory of God has departed.") But when these churches need a miracle, a word of knowledge, a word of wisdom, an intervention from the Lord, they will arise, shake themselves, and try to go out as before, only to discover that the Spirit of God has departed from them.

We in the Church of Jesus Christ need to shake and stir ourselves to make sure that the presence of the Lord has not departed from us.

God spoke to my own heart and told me, "I want you to come up higher. I want you to come up to another level. Take authority over yourself spiritually, mentally, physically, in every area, for there is a new plateau that is available to you."

If that is the Lord's word for you, then you will be out of His will if you choose to remain on the same spiritual plateau where you are now.

Samson Brought Low

But the Philistines took him, and put out his eyes, and brought him down to Gaza (the place of the strongholds)**, and *bound him* with fetters of brass; and he did grind in the prison house.**

Judges 16:21

The Body of Christ has been the target of many a comedian's jokes in these last few months. I believe that one of the reasons they have been so hard on us is because they were hoping that what we had was genuine. We have disappointed and hurt them. Now they are saying that Christianity is all sour grapes.

The reason they are doing so is because they have not separated the ministry from the man. Ministries are not men, and some of them have not ended up the way they started out.

Like Samson, some men and some ministries have been brought low. But this is not the end of the story.

7

Samson's Hair Grows Again!

The circle is complete. Samson has broken all of his Nazarite vows. Now he is like other men. But, thank God, it's not over!

Howbeit the hair of his head began to grow again after he was shaven.

Judges 16:22

The Body of Christ at this time is in transition. Some things appear to be somewhat unstable, but we are growing again. It takes time for hair to grow.

Samson Humiliated

Then the lords of the Philistines gathered them together for to offer a great sacrifice unto Dagon their (false) god, and to rejoice: for they said, Our god hath delivered Samson our enemy into our hand.

And when the people saw him, they praised their god: for they said, Our god hath delivered into our hands our enemy, and the destroyer of our country, which slew many of us.

And it came to pass, when their hearts were merry, that they said, Call for Samson, that he may make us sport. And they called for Samson out of the prison house; and he made them sport: and they set him between the pillars.

Judges 16:23-25

Samson was humiliated and stripped of his anointing and power. The Philistines made sport of him.

The same thing happens today when godly leaders fall. But the *good news* is, the game is *not* over!

Samson was about to make a comeback that would surpass all his previous exploits. The Spirit of God was about to come upon him for one final, massive triumph.

Samson's Final Triumph

And Samson said unto the lad that held him by the hand, Suffer me that I may feel the pillars whereupon the house standeth, that I may lean upon them.

Now the house was full of men and women; and all the lords of the Philistines were there; and there were upon the roof about three thousand men and women, that beheld while Samson made sport.

And Samson called unto the Lord, and said, O Lord God, remember me, I pray thee, only this once, O God, that I may be at once avenged of the Philistines for my two eyes.

And Samson took hold of the two middle pillars upon which the house stood, and on which it was borne up, of the one with his right hand, and of the other with his left.

And Samson said, Let me die with the Philistines. And he bowed himself with all his might; and the house fell upon the lords, and upon all the people that were therein. So the dead which he slew at his death were more than they which he slew in his life.

Judges 16:26-30

Samson made a mighty comeback, and the enemy did *not* prevail. Similarly, the Body of Christ in this hour is being awakened from sleep (lethargy) for a mighty comeback.

God's Message to the Church

. . . now it is high time to awake out of sleep: for *now* is our salvation nearer than when we believed.

The night is far spent, the day is at hand: let us therefore cast off the works of darkness, and let us put on the armour of light.

Let us walk honestly, as in the day; not in rioting and drunkenness, not in chambering and wantonness, not in strife and envying.

But put ye on the Lord Jesus Christ, *and make not provision for the flesh, to fulfil the lusts thereof.*
                                                    Romans 13:11-14

Friend, let's take heed to these words lest we, like Samson, rebel against God's command and taint the Kingdom of God and the precious name of Jesus.

Let's be a party to setting the stage for the glorious Church of Jesus Christ to go out in a blaze of glory!

The Harrison House Vision

Proclaiming the truth and the power
Of the Gospel of Jesus Christ
With excellence;

Challenging Christians to
Live victoriously,
Grow spiritually,
Know God intimately.

Harrison House
P. O. Box 35035
Tulsa, OK 74145

Additional Teaching
by David Crank

Tapes

The Spirit of Eli	$ 8.00
Humility	$ 8.00
Seeking the Lord	$ 8.00

Additional Financial Teaching
by David Crank

Books

Godly Finances and The Bible Way To Pay Off Your Home
(Foreword by Jerry Savelle)
Thousands are in print across America —
Write for your copy today $ 4.95

Tapes

How To Open the Windows of Heaven (4 tapes)	$16.00
The Hundredfold Return (3 tapes)	$12.00
The Bible Way to Get Out of Debt (2 tapes)	$ 8.00
How To Pay Off Your Home (6 tapes)	$24.00
The Bible Way to Make It Through the Winter (2 tapes)	$ 8.00
New Revelation in the Tithe (2 tapes)	$ 8.00
The Storehouse (2 tapes)	$ 8.00

David Crank conducts Holy Spirit and financial seminars across the U.S. For information concerning a seminar in your area, or to receive a complete teaching tape catalog, please write:

David Crank Ministries
1416 Larkin Williams Road
St. Louis, MO 63026
or call:
(314) 343-4359

Please feel free to contact the author with prayer requests or comments.